What Are Literature Pockets?

In *Literature Pockets—Fiction* the activities for each of the 12 genres are stored in a labeled pocket made from construction paper. (See directions below.) Add the charming cover and fasten the pockets together. Your students now have their own Fiction book to treasure.

How to Make the Pockets

1. Use a 12″ x 18″ (30.5 x 45.5 cm) piece of construction paper for each pocket. Fold up 6″ (15 cm) to make a 12″(30.5 cm) square.

2. Staple the right side of the pocket closed.

3. Punch two or three holes in the left side of the pocket.

4. Glue the title strip onto the pocket. The title strip is found on the bookmark page for each book.

5. Store each completed project in the pocket for that book.

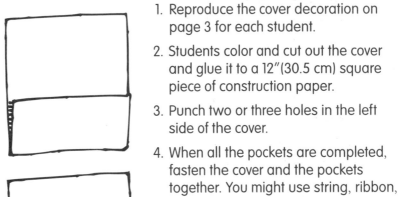

How to Make the Cover

1. Reproduce the cover decoration on page 3 for each student.

2. Students color and cut out the cover and glue it to a 12″(30.5 cm) square piece of construction paper.

3. Punch two or three holes in the left side of the cover.

4. When all the pockets are completed, fasten the cover and the pockets together. You might use string, ribbon, twine, raffia, or metal rings.

How to Use Literature Pockets
Fiction Genres

Basic Steps for Each Book

- Show several books from a genre. (Include any books that you have read aloud to the students or that they have read independently.) Summarize each of the books, and then ask students to identify similarities. Begin to build a list of attributes for the genre. As students read from the genre, refine the list.

- Make the genre bookmark. Have students cut out the bookmark and glue it to a 4″ x 11 1/2″ (10 x 29.5 cm) piece of construction paper. Review the description of the genre and the list of books. As you explore the genre in a pocket, send students to the library to see which books listed on the bookmark for that genre are available for them to read. (Students are asked to read at least two books in each genre.) They may add other titles they find to the blank lines on the bookmark.

- Complete the writing activities and art experiences provided for each genre pocket.

Realistic Fiction

Folklore

Adventure

Sports Stories

Science Fiction

Animal Stories

Mystery Stories

Jokes and Riddles

Historical Fiction

Poetry

Humorous Stories

Fantasy

Note: Reproduce this cover decoration for students to color, cut out, and glue to the cover of their Fiction book.

Name _____

Realistic Fiction

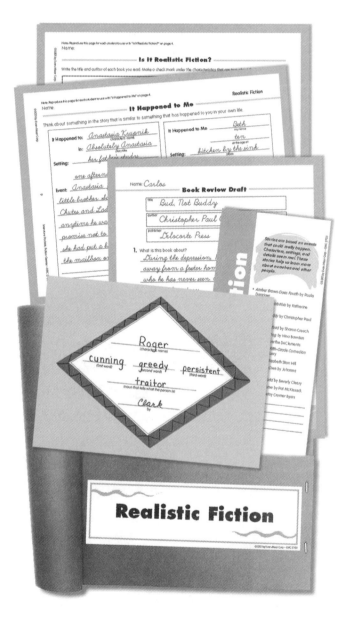

Realistic Fiction Bookmark .... page 5
Make the bookmark following the instructions on page 2. Review the description of the genre and the reading list provided on the bookmark. Then ask students to read at least two examples of realistic fiction.

Is It Realistic Fiction? .... page 6
Review the attributes of realistic fiction. Students list the books they read and then evaluate each book by checking the appropriate boxes on the form.

A Book Review .... pages 7 and 8
Students write a book review for one piece of realistic fiction they read.

It Happened to Me .... page 9
Ask students to find an event or situation in a realistic fiction book that is similar to something that has occurred in their own life. They then complete the form on page 9, comparing the event in the story with the event in their life.

Character Poem ....pages 10 and 11
Students create a short poem describing one character from a book of realistic fiction they have read.

Realistic Fiction

Stories are based on events that could really happen. Characters, settings, and details seem real. These stories help us learn more about ourselves and other people.

- *Amber Brown Goes Fourth* by Paula Danziger
- *Bridge to Terabithia* by Katherine Paterson
- *Bud, Not Buddy* by Christopher Paul Curtis
- *Chasing Redbird* by Sharon Creech
- *Granny the Pag* by Nina Bawden
- *Liar, Liar* by Barthe DeClements
- *My Life as a Fifth-Grade Comedian* by Elizabeth Levy
- *Bird Boy* by Elizabeth Starr Hill
- *Ozzie on His Own* by Johanna Hurwitz
- *Ramona's World* by Beverly Cleary
- *Run Away Home* by Pat McKissack
- *Tornado* by Betsy Cromer Byars

_____

_____

_____

_____

Realistic Fiction

Note: Reproduce this page for each student to use with "Is It Realistic Fiction?" on page 4.

Name: _____

Is It Realistic Fiction?

Write the title and author of each book you read. Make a check mark under the characteristics that are true about the book.

Name of Book	events could really happen	characters seem real	setting seems real	details seem real	learn about self and others
1 Title: _____ Author: _____					
2 Title: _____ Author: _____					
3 Title: _____ Author: _____					
4 Title: _____ Author: _____					
5 Title: _____ Author: _____					
6 Title: _____ Author: _____					

A Book Review

A book review expresses the reviewer's understanding of and opinion about a book he or she has read. The purpose of the review is to persuade other people to read or to avoid the book. Students write a review of a book of realistic fiction they have read.

Materials

- sample book reviews from newspapers or magazines
  (see *ALA Journal, Hornbook, Booklinks*, Amazon.com, etc., for reviews of children's books)
- page 8, reproduced for each student
- writing paper

Steps to Follow

1. Share several book reviews with the class. Analyze the reviews to see what types of information are included.

2. Brainstorm and make a list of the points to consider when writing the book review. Post the list in an accessible location.

   What is the book about?

   What is the basic subject of the book?

   Is there one part that seems really important?

   What is the book's theme or message?

   Why do you think the author wrote the book?

   What basic information or message does the author want to share?

   What does the reviewer like or dislike about the book?

   Are the characters interesting?

   Is the plot easy to follow?

   Does the book make good use of illustrations or other graphics?

3. Students select a realistic fiction book to read and review. Use the form on page 8 to create a rough draft of the review. Write the final copy on a sheet of writing paper.

Name: _____

Book Review Draft

title

author

publisher

1. What is this book about?

_____

_____

_____

_____

2. What is the book's message?

_____

_____

_____

3. Is this a book others should read? Why or why not? (Give specific examples.)

_____

_____

_____

_____

Realistic Fiction

Name: _____

It Happened to Me

Think about something in the story that is similar to something that has happened to you in your own life.

It Happened to Me

_____ my name

_____ at the age of

Setting:

_____ place

_____ time

Event:

_____

_____

_____

_____

_____

_____

_____

It Happened to

_____ character's name

in _____ story title

Setting

_____ place

_____ time

Event

_____

_____

_____

_____

_____

_____

_____

Character Poem

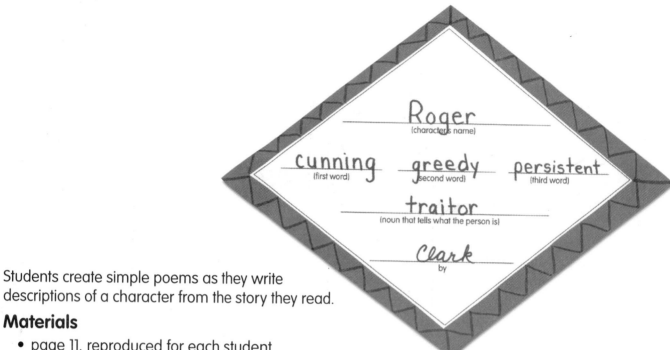

Students create simple poems as they write descriptions of a character from the story they read.

Materials

- page 11, reproduced for each student
- crayons, drawing pencils, or colored markers
- 9" x 12" (23 x 30.5 cm) construction paper

Steps to Follow

1. Discuss different types of descriptions—physical appearance, personality traits, talents, or strengths. Record these words on a chart or the chalkboard.

2. Choose a character from a familiar story. Model the process to follow in creating the character's description.

   character's name
   three descriptive words
   noun that tells what the character is

   Rewrite the description in an interesting way

3. Students select a character from the book they have read and, following the pattern above, write their descriptive poem.

4. Students cut out the poem and glue it to the sheet of construction paper. Cut around the poem leaving a border of colored paper. Decorate the border with a colorful design.

Roger
cunning, greedy, persistent
traitor

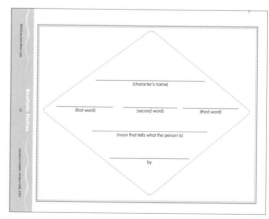

page 11

_____
(third word)

_____
(character's name)

_____
(second word)

_____
(noun that tells what the person is)

_____
by

_____
(first word)

Folklore

Folklore Bookmark........................... page 13
Make the bookmark following the instructions on page 2. Review the description of the genre and the reading list provided on the bookmark. Then ask students to read at least two examples of folklore.

Is It Folklore? .... page 14
Review the attributes of folklore. Students list the books they read, and then evaluate each book by checking the appropriate boxes on the form.

Folklore Mobile....................pages 15 and 16
Students create a book report mobile about one book of folklore they have read.

Make a Map............................pages 17–19
Students make a map representing a piece of folklore. The map will be used to portray the setting, characters, and events from the story.

Movable Puppet.................. pages 20 and 21
Students create a puppet of a main character from a story they read. The puppet will be hinged so it can move.

Folklore

Folklore stories reflect a culture. They are stories that were originally told aloud. They have been told over and over again, from generation to generation. Each time they are told, they may change a little.

- *And the Green Grass Grew All Around* by Alvin Schwartz
- *Cut from the Same Cloth* by Robert D. San Souci
- *Favorite Medieval Tales* by Mary Pope Osborne
- *Her Stories* by Virginia Hamilton
- *Jump On Over! The Adventures of Brer Rabbit and His Family* by Van Dyke Parks
- *Nursery Tales Around the World* by Judy Sierra
- *The Bronze Cauldron: Myths and Legends of the World* by Geraldine McCaughrean
- *The Dragon Prince: A Chinese Beauty and The Beast Tale* by Laurence Yep
- *The Rough-Face Girl* by Rafe Martin
- *Three Sacks of Truth* by Eric Kimmel
- *When the Chenoo Howls* by Joseph and James Bruchac
- *With a Whoop and a Holler: A Bushel of Lore from Way Down South* by Nancy Van Laan

_____

_____

_____

_____

Folklore

Note: Reproduce this page for each student to use with "Is It Folklore?" on page 12.

Name: _____

Is It Folklore?

Write the title and author of each book you read. Make a check mark under the characteristics that are true about the book.

Name of Book	a story about a time long ago	story gives detail about the culture in which it was set	a version of a story you've heard before (Name it)
1 Title: _____ Author: _____			
2 Title: _____ Author: _____			
3 Title: _____ Author: _____			
4 Title: _____ Author: _____			
5 Title: _____ Author: _____			
6 Title: _____ Author: _____			

Folklore Mobile

Students share the stories they read by making simple mobiles.

Materials

- page 16, reproduced for each student
- 2″ x 17″ (5 x 43 cm) tagboard
- construction paper scraps
- nine 12″ (30.5 cm) pieces of string
- crayons or marking pens
- ruler
- hole punch
- Optional: quart-sized self-locking plastic bags

Steps to Follow

1. Discuss the types of items that must be included on the mobile (title, author, and illustrator of book; main characters; main events of the story). Explain that pictures and/or words may be used.

2. Pass out materials or provide a central collection point.

3. Guide students through these steps to prepare their mobiles:

   a. Measure, mark, and punch holes in the tagboard as shown.

   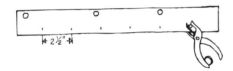

   b. Write the title, author, and illustrator of the book on the strip.

   c. Staple the strip end to end to form a ring. Tie a string to each of the six bottom holes. (You may punch more holes if you need to hang more than six items from the mobile.)

   d. Illustrate the main characters from the story on the oval shapes (page 16). Write each character's name on the oval.

   e. Write the main events from the plot on the rectangles.

   f. Cut out the shapes and glue them to construction paper scraps. Cut around the shapes, leaving a narrow border. Punch a hole in the top of each shape.

   g. Tie a string from each of the three top holes. Bring the strings together and tie a knot. Now the mobile can be hung.

4. After students prepare their mobiles, provide time for them to share their work and then place the mobiles in their pockets. (The mobiles may be put into quart-sized self-locking plastic bags to keep the pieces from being damaged.)

Folklore Mobile

Name:

Name:

Name:

Literature Pockets—Fiction • EMC 2703

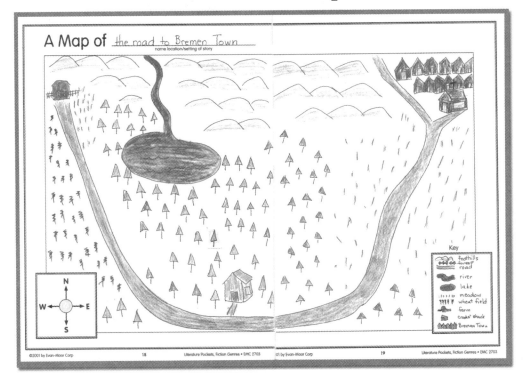

Students make individual maps representing folklore they read.

Materials

- pages 18 and 19, reproduced for each student
- crayons, colored pencils, or marking pens
- glue
- scissors
- ruler
- writing paper

Steps to Follow

1. Students recall and write details about the setting and events in the book of folklore they read.

2. Cut out and glue pages 18 and 19 together to make the blank map.

3. Draw the setting (woods, town, etc.) of the story. This could be a single setting such as the woods in *Goldilocks and The Three Bears* or a whole landscape of fields, forests, and towns in a story such as *Saint George and the Dragon.*

4. Complete the key in the corner to show symbols for the trees, landforms, and buildings, etc., used on the map.

5. Add characters from the story engaged in some activity from the plot.

Folklore

A Map of _____
name location/setting of story

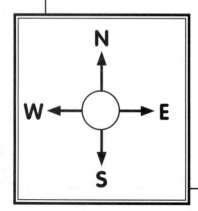

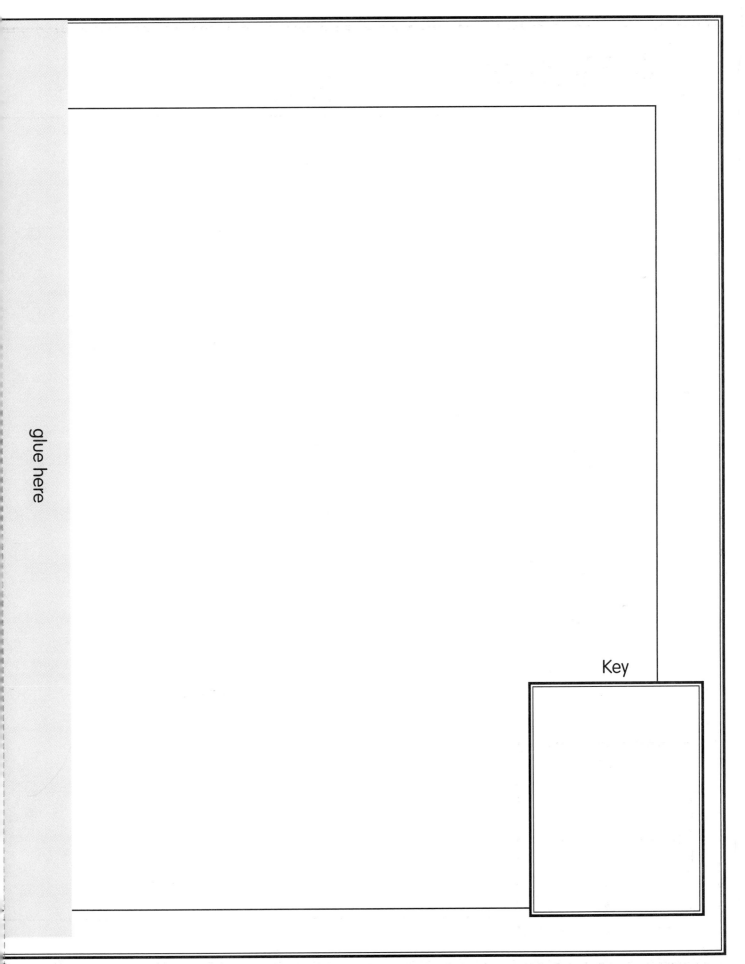

glue here

Key

Movable Puppet

Students select a character from the story they read and make a puppet of that character. They then manipulate the puppet as they retell the folktale.

Materials

- 12″ x 18″ (30.5 x 45.5 cm) tagboard (or use old file folders)
- page 21, reproduced for each student
- paper fasteners
- 2 plastic straws or thin doweling
- crayons or marking pens
- scissors
- hole punch
- cellophane tape

Steps to Follow

1. Cut out the templates on page 21. Trace around the templates on the tagboard.

2. Lightly sketch the character on tagboad.

3. Color and cut out the pieces.

4. Punch holes where needed. Attach the movable parts with paper fasteners. Tape the paper fastener on the back of the figure to hold it in place.

5. Tape straws or doweling to the puppet— one piece to the body, one piece to the movable part.

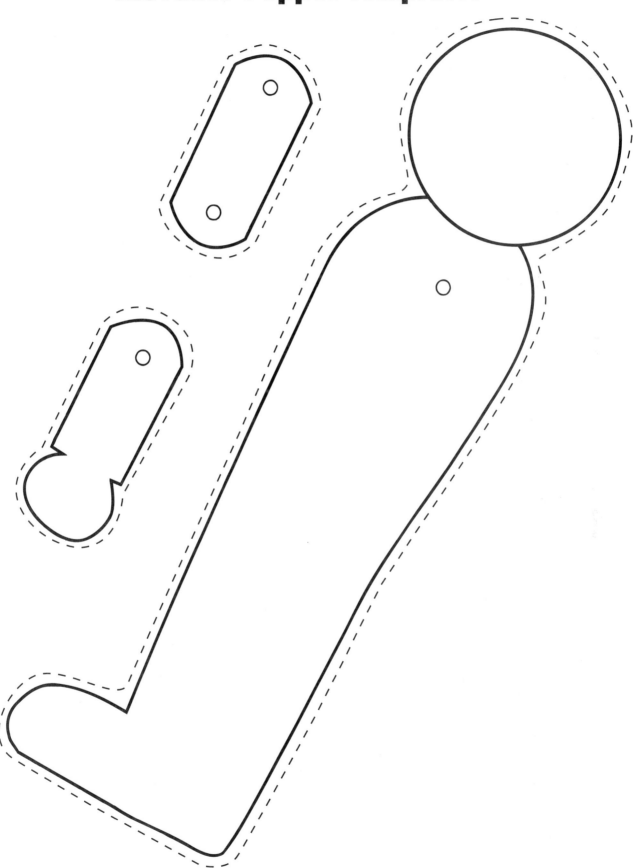

Literature Pockets—Fiction • EMC 2703

Adventure

Make the bookmark following the instructions on page 2. Review the description of the genre and the reading list provided on the bookmark. Then ask students to read at least two examples of adventure stories.

Review the attributes of adventure stories. Students list the books they read and then evaluate each book by checking the appropriate boxes on the form.

Students make paper "backpacks." They then fill the backpack with the items that would be needed for the adventure they read about.

Students complete a journal as though it were being written by one of the main characters in the story.

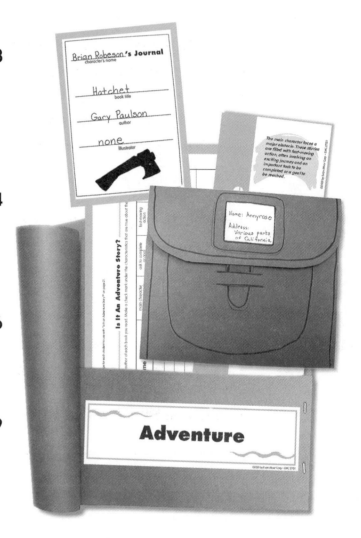

Literature Pockets—Fiction • EMC 2703

Adventure

The main character faces a major obstacle. These stories are filled with fast-moving action, often involving an exciting journey and an important task to be completed or a goal to be reached.

- *Alice Rose and Sam* by Kathryn Lasky
- *Bandit's Moon* by Sid Fleischman
- *Bearstone* by Will Hobbs
- *By Truck to the North: My Winter Adventure* by Pearson Turnball
- *Call Me Francis Tucket* by Gary Paulsen
- *Hatchet* by Gary Paulsen
- *Hob and the Peddler* by Willia Mayne
- *Jackaroo* by Cynthia Voigt
- *Night of the Twisters* by Ivy Ruckman
- *Pathki Nana: Kootenai Girl* by Kenneth Thomasma
- *Robin's Country* by Monica Furlong
- *The Firework-Maker's Daughter* by Philip Pullman
- *Treehouse Tales* by Anne Isaacs

_____

_____

_____

_____

Adventure

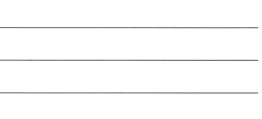

Note: Reproduce this page for each student to use with "Is It an Adventure Story?" on page 22.

Name: _____

Is It an Adventure Story?

Write the title and author of each book you read. Make a check mark under the characteristics that are true about the book.

Name of Book	main character faces an obstacle (Name the obstacle)	task to complete or goal to reach	fast-moving action	exciting journey
1 Title: _____ Author: _____				
2 Title: _____ Author: _____				
3 Title: _____ Author: _____				
4 Title: _____ Author: _____				
5 Title: _____ Author: _____				
6 Title: _____ Author: _____				

What's in Your Backpack?

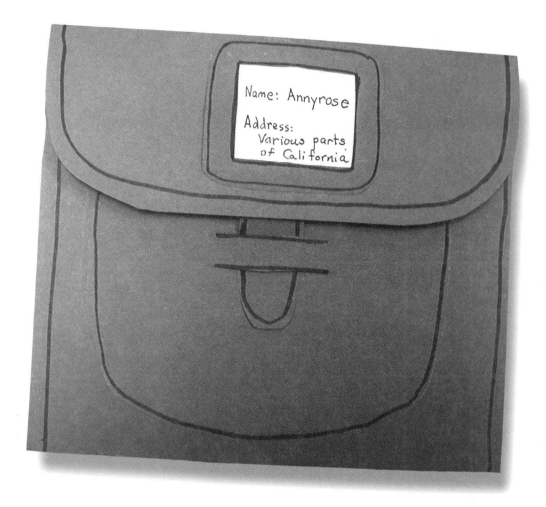

Students make a backpack and then fill it with items they would take on the adventure in the story they read.

Materials

- brown construction paper for the following:
     backpack and strap—8" x 18" (20 x 45.5 cm)
     pocket—4" x 6" (10 x 15 cm)
     nameplate—2 1/2" x 3" (6.5 x 7.5 cm)
- 2" x 3" (5 x 7.5 cm) white construction paper
- 2" x 3" (5 x 7.5 cm) piece of laminating film or plastic wrap
- tape
- black crayons or marking pens
- glue
- scissors
- ruler

Steps to Follow

1. Cut a 1" (2.5 cm) strip from one end of the large brown construction paper. Then cut 4" (10 cm) off the strip to use for the backpack strap. Round the corners of the strap at one end. Outline the strap in black. Save the strap to attach once the rest of the backpack is completed.

2. Round off two corners of one end of the large piece of brown construction paper. Fold the rounded end down 3" (7.5 cm) to make the backpack flap. Outline the flap in black.

3. Fold the bottom of the construction paper up to the flap fold to complete the basic backpack.

4. Using the 4" x 6" (10 x 15 cm) brown construction paper, make the pocket. Round two corners of the pocket. Fold it gently in half and cut two parallel slits near the top edge for the strap to go through. Open the pocket and glue it about 1/2" (1.25 cm) from the bottom edge of the backpack, leaving the top edge open.

5. Using the 2 1/2" x 3" (6.5 x 7.5 cm) brown paper, make the nameplate. Round all four corners. Gently fold the nameplate in half. Cut out a window. Unfold the nameplate and tape the laminating film to the backside of the window. Write "Name" and "Address" on the white paper. Tape the name paper inside the window. Outline the nameplate in black and glue it to the backpack flap.

6. To judge where the strap should be attached to the flap, insert the strap in the slit of the pocket. Fold the flap over the top of the pocket and glue or tape the strap to the inside of the flap.

7. Open the backpack. Draw and/or list all the items that would be packed for the adventure in the story.

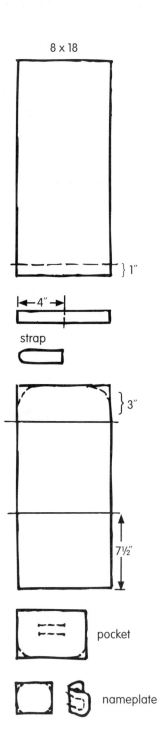

Adventure

An Adventure Journal

Students complete a book report in journal format.

Materials

- 12" x 18" (30.5 x 45.5 cm) colored construction paper
- page 28, reproduced for each student
- page 29, three copies reproduced for each student
- scissors
- crayons or marking pens
- pencil
- glue

Steps to Follow—Basic Book

Guide students through these steps:

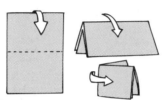

1. Fold the construction paper as shown.

2. Open the paper and cut on the fold as shown, stopping at the horizontal fold.

3. Fold in half lengthwise. Push in the ends. "Poof," and you have a minibook.

Steps to Follow—Journal

1. Explain to students that they are to select a main character from the adventure story they read, and then write a summary following a journal format.

2. Prepare the front and back covers.

3. Write these guidelines on the chalkboard and discuss them with students:

    page 1—Have the character introduce him or herself.

    pages 2 through 5—Write journal entries about events from the story in the order in which they occurred.

    page 6—End with how the character felt about the adventure.

4. Cut apart the writing forms. Glue the front and back covers to the book. Then glue a journal page to each of the four inside pages. Allow the glue to dry before writing. (This is a good time to think about what to write on each page.)

5. Complete the journal pages. Encourage students to return to the book to refresh their memory of events as necessary. Fill in the evaluation checklist on the outside back cover.

Adventure

An Adventure Journal

cover

back cover

's Journal

_____
character's name

_____
book title

_____
author

_____
illustrator

Book Evaluation

by _____
(your name)

☐ It kept me on the edge
of my seat!

☐ It was pretty exciting.

☐ It was okay, but nothing
special.

☐ It wasn't worth reading.

Adventure

An Adventure Journal

inside pages

date

_____

date

_____

Sports Stories

Sports Stories Bookmark .... **page 31**
Make the bookmark following the instructions on page 2. Review the description of the genre and the reading list provided on the bookmark. Then ask the students to read at least two sports stories.

Is It a Sports Story? .... **page 32**
Review the attributes of sports stories. Students list the books they read and then evaluate each book by checking the appropriate boxes on the form.

Cross-Legged Player .... **pages 33–35**
After creating a cross-legged sports figure, students fill the pockets with "Who, What, Where, When, Why" facts about the story they read.

The Winner Is... .... **pages 36–38**
Students create original stories about a winning person or team, using their own favorite sport as the theme for the story. Each finished story is placed in a medal-shaped cover.

Sports Stories

Some or all of the story elements—characters, setting, problem, solution, and events—are based on some kind of sport. The story may have other elements, but sports is the main ingredient.

- *Above the Rim* by Hank Herman
- *Arthur Makes the Team* by Stephen Krensky and Marc Tolon Brown
- *Baseball Fever* by Johanna Hurwitz
- *Game Plan* by Thomas Dygard
- *Great Lengths* by Sandra Diersch
- *Home Run Hero* by Dean Hughes
- *In the Year of the Boar and Jackie Robinson* by Bette Lord
- *Mikayla's Victory* by Cynthia Bates
- *On Guard* by Donna Jo Napoli
- *Skinnybones* by Barbara Park
- *Stranger in Right Field* by Matt Christopher
- *Woodsie* by Bruce Brooks

_____

_____

_____

_____

Sports Stories

©2001 by Evan-Moor Corp. • EMC 2703

Note: Reproduce this page for each student to use with "Is It a Sports Story?" on page 30.

Name: _____

Is It a Sports Story?

Write the title and author of each book you read. Make a check mark under the characteristics that are true about the book.

Name of Book	sports characters	sports setting	problem & solution revolve around sports
1 Title: _____ Author: _____			
2 Title: _____ Author: _____			
3 Title: _____ Author: _____			
4 Title: _____ Author: _____			
5 Title: _____ Author: _____			
6 Title: _____ Author: _____			

Literature Pockets—Fiction • EMC 2703

Cross-Legged Player

After making simple cross-legged sports figures, students use the 5 W's to recall events from the sports story they read.

Materials

- construction paper for the following:
    body—9″ (23 cm) square (colors appropriate to the sport or team)
    head—3″ (7.5 cm) square (a skin color)
    hands—1″ (2.5 cm) square (skin color)
- construction paper scraps
- scissors
- glue
- stapler
- crayons

Steps to Follow—Player

1. The colors selected for the basic shape should be appropriate for the sport or team of the player in the story. Begin with the 9″ (23 cm) square of construction paper. Follow the steps to the right.

a. Fold the paper in half, corner to corner, then reopen.

b. Fold the paper in to the center line.

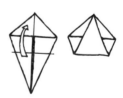

c. Fold the narrow point up to the top point.

d. Open the paper and cut up the center line. Stop in the middle. Cut other lines as shown.

e. Refold the paper and cross the legs.

f. Pull out the pocket. Staple the legs and pocket.

Sports Stories

2. Using the skin-colored paper, make the head and hands as shown. Add details with crayons.

3. Add other details such as a cap, team insignia, or sports equipment using construction paper scraps and crayons.

 head

 hands

Steps to Follow—5 W's

1. Using the form on page 35, students answer the following questions about the story they read.

> **Who** is the story about?
>
> **What** happened?
>
> **Where** did it happen?
>
> **When** did it happen?
>
> **Why** did it happen?

page 35

2. After answering the questions, cut the paper apart and place the pieces inside the pocket of the cross-legged player.

Note: To place the figure in the Sports pocket, gently push in the pocket and bend up the legs.

_____

(title of story)

Who? _____

_____

_____

What? _____

_____

_____

Where? _____

_____

_____

When? _____

_____

_____

Why? _____

_____

_____

The Winner Is...

Students write original stories about a winning person or team using their favorite sport as the theme for the story. Each finished story is placed in a cover shaped like a medal.

Materials

- page 37, reproduced for each student
- page 38, reproduced on white construction paper for each student
- 9" x 12" (23 x 30.5 cm) white construction paper
- writing paper, cut using medal pattern on page 37
- scissors
- glue
- marking pens

Steps to Follow—Medal Book Cover

1. Color and cut out the medal form to make the front cover for the story. Draw a picture in the circle to represent the sport or the winner. Trace the medal on white construction paper and cut it out to make the back cover.

2. When the story is completed, staple the pages inside the cover.

Steps to Follow—Story

1. Review with students the steps in writing a story. Ask students to think about these elements:

   Who are the **characters** going to be?

   What is the **setting** going to be? Remind them that this is the location and the time of the story.

   Who is telling the story—one of the main characters or an onlooker?

   What **events** or problems will occur in the story?

   What will the climactic event be?

   How will the story end?

   Remind students that their stories need a **beginning** that establishes characters and setting, a **middle** that describes events, and an **ending** that makes sense in relation to the rest of the story.

2. Using page 38, students plan their sports stories. They write their final drafts on writing paper cut into circles to fit inside the medal cover.

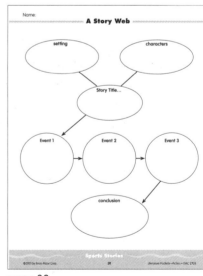

page 38

THE WINNER IS...

by

A Story Web

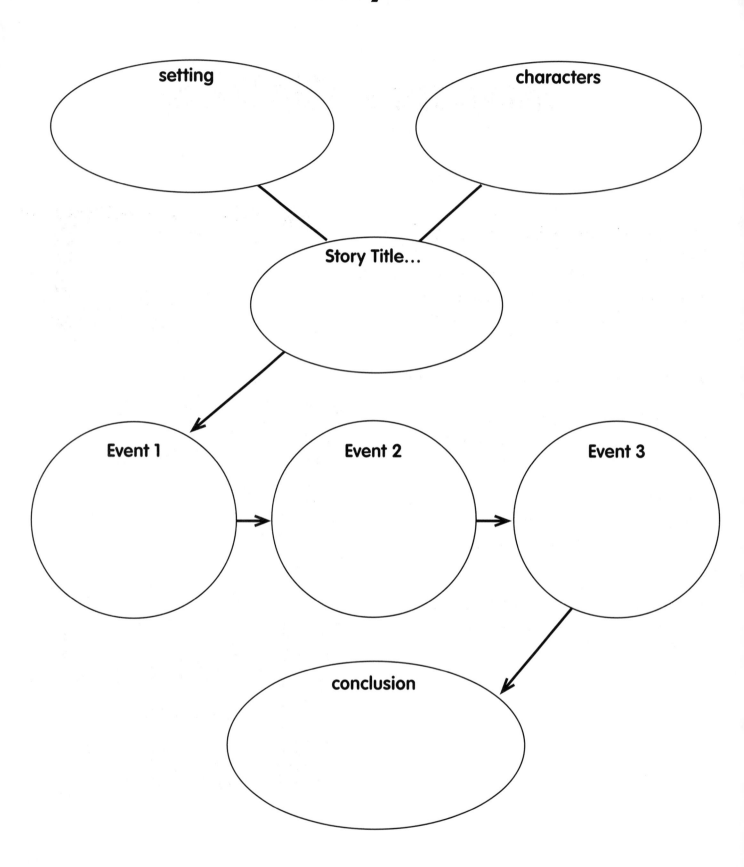

setting

characters

Story Title...

Event 1

Event 2

Event 3

conclusion

   Literature Pockets—Fiction • EMC 2703

Science Fiction

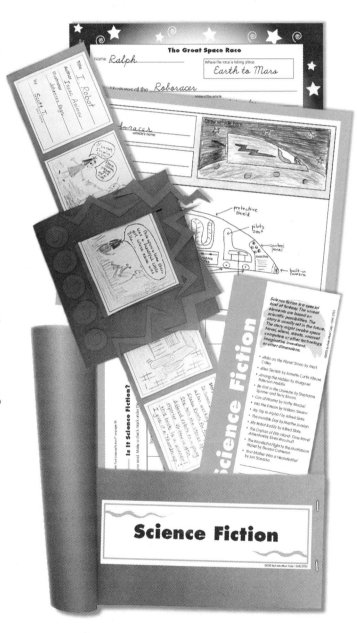

Science Fiction Bookmark .... **page 40**
Make the bookmark following the instructions on page 2. Review the description of the genre and the reading list provided on the bookmark. Then ask students to read at least two examples of science fiction.

Is It Science Fiction? .... **page 41**
Review the attributes of science fiction stories. Students list the books they read and then evaluate each book by checking the appropriate boxes on the form.

Sci Fi TV .... **pages 42 and 43**
Students report on a science fiction book by making a "television show" of the story.

Space Race .... **pages 44–46**
Students imagine living in the far-distant future and design a vehicle for the great "Space Race."

Science Fiction

Science fiction is a special kind of fantasy. The unreal elements are based on scientific possibilities. The story is usually set in the future. The story might involve space travel, aliens, robots, unusual computers or other technology, imaginative inventions, or other dimensions.

©2001 by Evan-Moor Corp. • EMC 2703

- *Akiko on the Planet Smoo* by Mark Crilley
- *Alien Secrets* by Annette Curtis Klause
- *Among the Hidden* by Margaret Paterson Haddix
- *Be First in the Universe* by Stephanie Spinner and Terry Bisson
- *Can of Worms* by Kathy Mackel
- *Into the Dream* by William Sleator
- *My Trip to Alpha I* by Alfred Slote
- *The Invisible Day* by Marthe Jocelyn
- *My Robot Buddy* by Alfred Slote
- *The Orphan of Ellis Island: A Time-travel Adventure* by Elvira Woodruff
- *The Wonderful Flight to the Mushroom Planet* by Eleanor Cameron
- *Your Mother Was a Neanderthal* by Jon Scieszka

_____

_____

_____

_____

Science Fiction

©2001 by Evan-Moor Corp. • EMC 2703

Name: _____

Is It Science Fiction?

Write the title and author of each book you read. Make a check mark under the characteristics that are true about the book.

Name of Book	based on scientific possibilities	set in future or another dimension	space travel	robotic or alien characters
1 Title: _____ Author: _____				
2 Title: _____ Author: _____				
3 Title: _____ Author: _____				
4 Title: _____ Author: _____				
5 Title: _____ Author: _____				
6 Title: _____ Author: _____				

Students design a futuristic or alien television screen to hold the pull-through strip to report on the science fiction book they read.

Materials

- page 43, reproduced for each student
- 6" x 12" (15 x 30.5 cm) construction paper
- 4" x 18" (10 x 45.5 cm) construction paper
- crayons, colored pencils, or marking pens
- scissors
- cellophane tape
- Exacto® knife (for adult or supervised use only)
- assorted materials for decorating the television set: aluminum foil, pipe cleaners, glitter, star and moon stickers, etc.
- writing paper

Steps to Follow—TV Set

1. Cut slits in the 6" x 12" (15 x 30.5 cm) construction paper as shown. Fold the paper in half and tape the bottom together.

2. Using imagination and a variety of materials, decorate the television set to give it a futuristic or alien appearance.

3. Cut out the six squares on page 43. Glue them to the long strip beginning with the title box and ending with the evaluation box.

Steps to Follow—Pull-through TV Show

1. Using the writing paper, students list in sequence the major events in the story they read. They circle the four events they wish to show on the pull-through strip.

2. Students complete the title and evaluation boxes. They then draw one scene in each remaining box. Captions or speech bubbles may be added where necessary to move the plot along.

3. Slip the completed paper strip into the TV set. Pull it through to tell the story.

Science Fiction

Title
_____

Author
_____

Illustrator
_____

by
_____
        your name

Story Evaluation

_____
_____
_____
_____
_____
_____
_____
_____

Space Race

What will vehicles for a great race through space in the far-distant future be like? Here's the opportunity to find out what your students think.

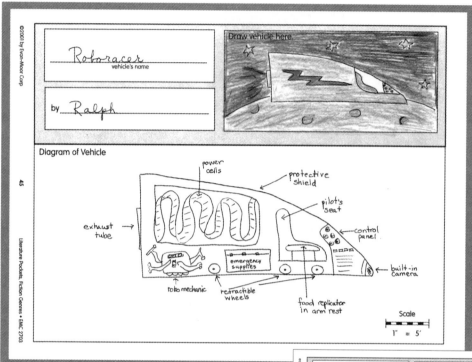

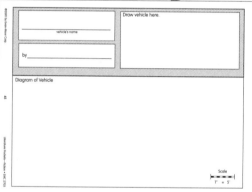

Materials

- pages 45 and 46, reproduced for each student
- crayons or colored pencils

Steps to Follow

1. Ask students to imagine that they live far in the future. They have been invited to take part in a great space race. They are to design a vehicle for the race.

2. Discuss what type of race this "Space Race" might be. Where might it take place—on a distant planet, among the stars, throughout our solar system? What kinds of special adaptations would be needed in different locations? What might the vehicles look like?

3. Students decide where their vehicle will race. They then draw a picture of the vehicle in the smaller box on page 45. They use the rest of the page to draw a detailed diagram of the vehicle, labeling the parts and features.

4. Using page 46, students complete a descriptive paragraph describing where the race will take place and also the special features of their vehicle that will allow it to win the race.

Science Fiction

Draw vehicle here.

vehicle's name

by

Diagram of Vehicle

Scale
1″ = 5′

The Great Space Race

Name: _____

Where the race is taking place:

name of the vehicle

Special features of the _____

Literature Pockets—Fiction • EMC 2703

Animal Stories

Animal Stories Bookmark .... page 48
Make the bookmark following the instructions on page 2. Review the description of the genre and the reading list provided on the bookmark. Then ask students to read at least two animal stories.

Is It an Animal Story? .... page 49
Review the attributes of animal stories. Students list the books they read and then evaluate each book by checking the appropriate boxes on the form.

Mapping the Story .... page 50
Students report on an animal story by creating a story map using the form on page 50.

Animal Paper Chains.......... pages 51 and 52
Students make a chain of an animal character from a story they have read. They write a characteristic of or fact about the animal on each section of the chain. Page 52 contains animal templates that may be used by the students, or they may create their own.

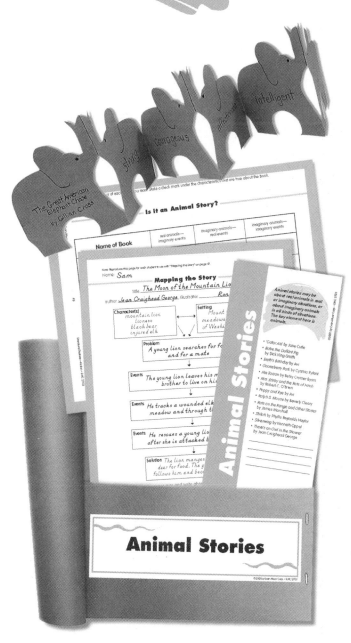

Animal Stories

Animal stories may be about real animals in real or imaginary situations, or about imaginary animals in all kinds of situations. The key element here is animals.

- *'Gator Aid* by Jane Cutler
- *Babe the Gallant Pig* by Dick King-Smith
- *Ereth's Birthday* by Avi
- *Gooseberry Park* by Cynthia Rylant
- *Me Tarzan* by Betsy Cromer Byars
- *Mrs. Frisby and the Rats of Nimh* by Robert C. O'Brien
- *Poppy and Rye* by Avi
- *Ralph S. Mouse* by Beverly Cleary
- *Rats on the Range and Other Stories* by James Marshall
- *Shiloh* by Phyllis Reynolds Naylor
- *Silverwing* by Kenneth Oppel
- *There's an Owl in the Shower* by Jean Craighead George

_____

_____

_____

_____

Animal Stories

Name: _____

Is It an Animal Story?

Write the title and author of each book you read. Make a check mark under the characteristics that are true about the book.

Name of Book	real animals— imaginary events	imaginary animals— real events	imaginary animals— imaginary events
1 Title: _____ Author: _____			
2 Title: _____ Author: _____			
3 Title: _____ Author: _____			
4 Title: _____ Author: _____			
5 Title: _____ Author: _____			
6 Title: _____ Author: _____			

Literature Pockets—Fiction • EMC 2703

Name:

Mapping the Story

Title _____

Author _____ Illustrator _____

Character(s)	Setting

Problem

Event

Event

Event

Solution

Turn this paper over and write about the best part of this book.

Animal Paper Chains

Students select a character from an animal story and make an animal chain to use in the following writing activity.

Materials

- reproduce page 52 (you will need enough copies for each student to have one animal)
- two 5" x 27" (13 x 68.5 cm) pieces of butcher paper
- scissors
- paper clips
- ruler
- pencil or pen

Steps to Follow

1. Practice the process of cutting an animal chain using an animal template from page 52. Students will follow the same basic steps when they create their own animals.

   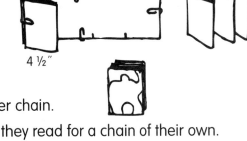

   a. Measure 4 1/2" (11 cm) sections on one of the butcher paper strips.

   b. Accordion fold the strip. Use paper clips to hold the sections still while cutting.

   c. Give each student one animal template. They trace the template on the first (top) section of the folded paper.

   d. Cut out the animal, being careful to leave an entire folded edge uncut.

   e. Open the animal carefully to see the paper chain.

2. Next, students select an animal from the story they read for a chain of their own. After folding the paper, they sketch the animal on the first section. Remind them to be sure to touch the fold on both sides. Then they cut out their animal.

3. After opening up the chain, students write the name of the animal story and its author on the first animal in the chain. Then they write one of the following on each animal:

   a fact about the animal

   a characteristic of the animal

   an event from the story

Animal Stories

Animal Templates

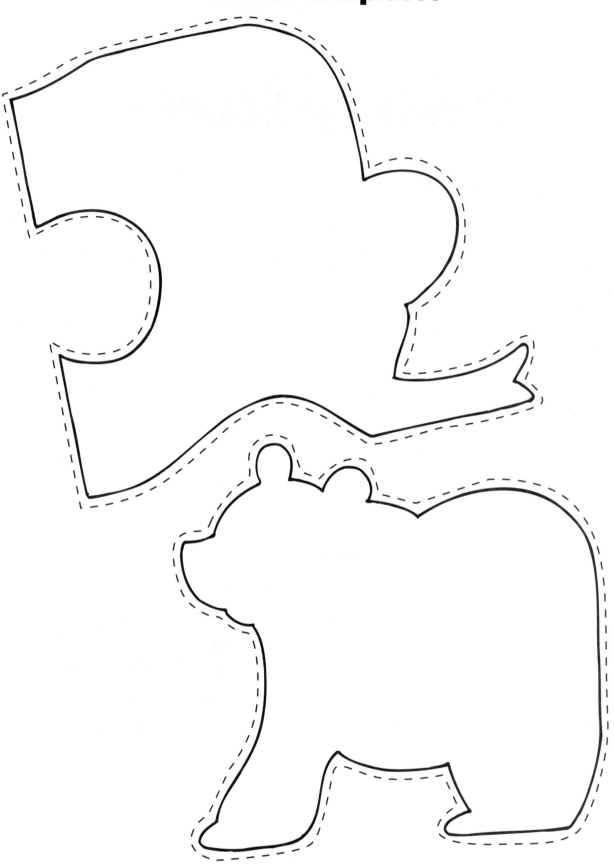

Mystery Stories

Make the bookmark following the instructions on page 2. Review the description of the genre and the reading list provided on the bookmark. Then ask students to read at least two mystery stories.

Review the attributes of mystery stories. Students list the books they read and then evaluate each book by checking the appropriate boxes on the form.

After students make a magnifying glass such as a detective might use, they write a summary and evaluation of their mystery.

Students fill this folding box with clues that gradually reveal the perpetrator of the crime in the mystery. Students write clues on the flaps of the box, leading to the name of the guilty party written in the center of the box.

Mystery Stories

A mystery story is filled with suspense and contains a problem or a crime to solve. The plot contains the clues that lead to the solution. The story usually contains the person doing the detective work, a victim, a wrongdoer, and other suspects who are found to be innocent. Unexpected and imaginative events and settings add to the suspense in a mystery story.

©2001 by Evan-Moor Corp • EMC 2703

- *Behind the Attic Wall* by Sylvia Cassedy
- *The Bomb at the Bessledorf Bus Depot* by Phyllis Reynolds Naylor
- *Bunnicula: A Rabbit-Tale of Mystery* by Deborah Howe
- *Cam Jansen and the Ghostly Mystery* by David Adler
- *Coffin On a Case* by Eve Bunting
- *The Dark Stairs* by Betsy Cromer Byars
- *Encyclopedia Brown and the Case of the Two Spies* by Donald Sobol
- *Kidnap at the Catfish Café* by Patricia Reilly Giff
- *The Case of the Goblin Pearls* by Laurence Yep
- *The Curse of the Blue Figurine* by John Bellairs
- *The Light on Hogback Hill* by Cynthia DeFelice
- *Too Many Secrets* by Betty Ren Wright

_____

_____

_____

_____

Mystery Stories

©2001 by Evan-Moor Corp • EMC 2703

Name: _____

Is It a Mystery Story?

Write the title and author of each book you read. Make a check mark under the characteristics that are true about the book.

Name of Book	problem or crime to solve	protagonist solves mystery	clues provided	wrongdoer	innocent suspects
1 Title: _____ Author: _____					
2 Title: _____ Author: _____					
3 Title: _____ Author: _____					
4 Title: _____ Author: _____					
5 Title: _____ Author: _____					
6 Title: _____ Author: _____					

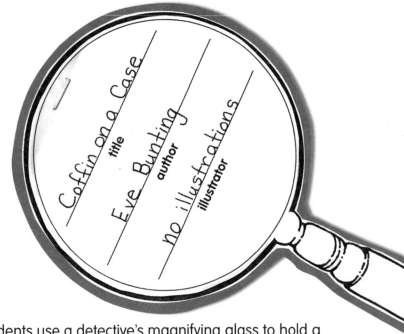

Students use a detective's magnifying glass to hold a summary and an evaluation of the mystery story they read.

Materials

- pages 57 and 58, reproduced for each student
- 6" x 9 1/2" (15 x 24.5 cm) card stock (old file folders may be used)
- black marking pen
- scissors
- 5" (13 cm) square of clear plastic
- stapler

Steps to Follow

1. Cut out the magnifying glass and glue it on the card stock. Cut around the magnifying glass, leaving a narrow border of color.

2. Cut out the circles on page 58. Trace one circle on the plastic square and cut it out.

3. Fill in the circles to summarize and evaluate the mystery story that was read. (Provide extra circles cut from lined paper for students who need more writing room.)

4. Arrange the circles in order, place the plastic circle on top, and staple them to the magnifying glass.

page 57

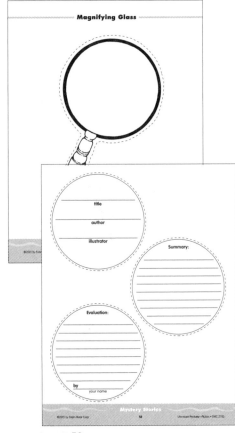

page 58

Mystery Stories

57 Literature Pockets—Fiction • EMC 2703

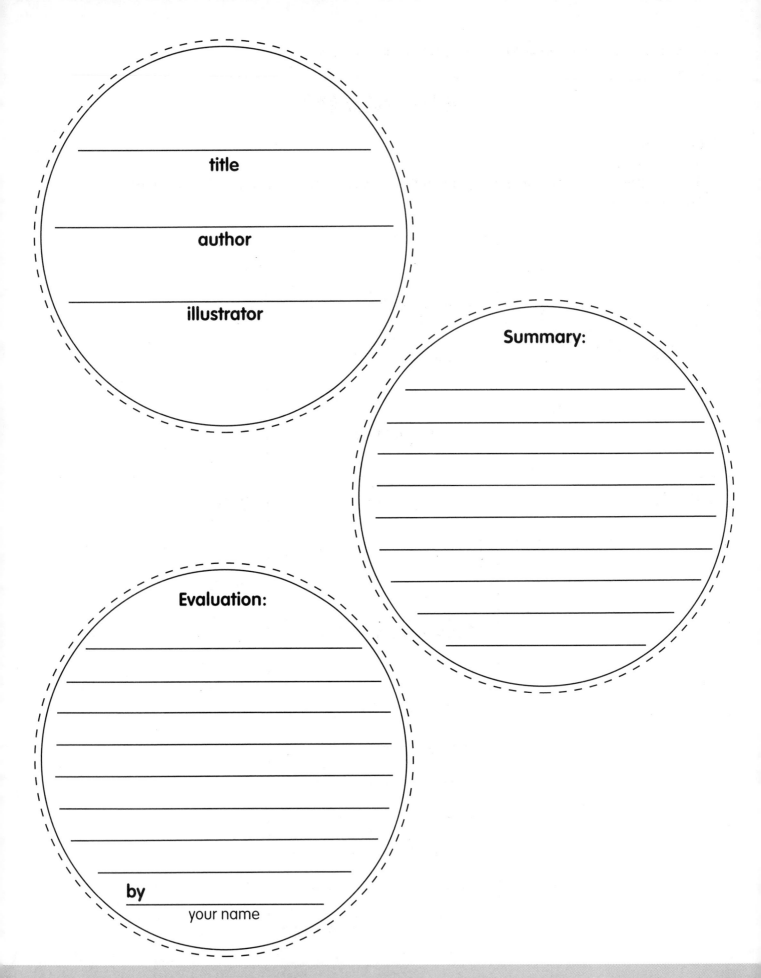

title

author

illustrator

Summary:

Evaluation:

by _____
your name

Name:

Who Did It?

1. Cut out the form.
2. Fill in each box.
3. Turn the paper over and write the name of the story character "who did it" in the center box.
4. Fold on the fold lines.

Garth

Write your name here.

author

title

Who Did It?

Clue 3:

_____

_____

_____

_____

fold 4 ▲

fold 1 ◄

Write your name here.

fold 2 ►

fold 3 ▼

Clue 2:

_____

_____

_____

_____

_____

_____

_____

_____

Clue 1:

Jokes and Riddles

Jokes and Riddles Bookmark .... page 61
Make the bookmark following the instructions on page 2. Review the description of the genre and the reading list provided on the bookmark. Then ask students to read at least two joke and riddle books.

Is It a Joke or Riddle Book?.............. page 62
Review the attributes of joke and riddle books. Students list the books they read and then evaluate each book by checking the appropriate boxes on the form.

It Tickled My Funny Bone .... pages 63 and 64
Students write joke or riddle book reports on a series of "funny bones."

Riddles—A Flap Book .... pages 65 and 66
Students lift the flaps of this minibook to find the answers to each other's favorite riddles.

The Little Book of Great Jokes .... page 67
Students make one more little book—this time to contain the four greatest jokes they know.

Jokes and Riddles

Jokes are very short stories designed to make people laugh. The humor is often at the end of the joke.

Riddles pose a question or a problem. They are to be puzzling, misleading, or mystifying. Riddles are often presented as a guessing game.

_____

_____

_____

_____

Jokes and Riddles

©2001 by Evan-Moor Corp • EMC 2703

Name: _____

Is It a Joke or a Riddle Book?

Write the title and author of each book you read. Make a check mark under the characteristics that are true about the book.

Name of Book	jokes and riddles	only riddles	only jokes	funny	challenging puzzles
1 Title: _____ Author: _____					
2 Title: _____ Author: _____					
3 Title: _____ Author: _____					
4 Title: _____ Author: _____					
5 Title: _____ Author: _____					
6 Title: _____ Author: _____					

title: A Pocketful of Laughter

author: Joanna Cole and Stephanie Calmenson

illustrator: Marilyn Hafner

Each funny bone contains part of the students' reports on a joke or riddle book.

Materials

- page 64, reproduced for each student
- 3" x 8" (7.5 x 20 cm) black construction paper
- scissors
- glue
- stapler

Steps to Follow

1. Cut out the bones on page 64. Complete the task on each bone.

2. Arrange the bones in order and staple them to the black construction paper.

3. Trim the black paper to create a black border around the bones.

page 64

title: _____

author: _____

illustrator: _____

What I liked about this book:

_____

_____

_____

What I didn't like about this book:

_____

_____

_____

Rate this book—Did it tickle your funny bone?

funniest thing I ever read   laughed a few times

very funny   BORING

Jokes and Riddles

Students make this little flap book of their favorite riddles to share with their classmates.

Materials

- page 66, two copies reproduced for each student
- 3" x 10" (7.5 x 25.5 cm) construction paper
- scissors
- glue
- crayons

Steps to Follow

1. Cut out the flap patterns on the dotted lines. Fold on the fold line to make the flap. The folded flap should be on the right side of the page.

2. Write a riddle on each lined section.

3. Open up the flap and draw or write the answer to the riddle underneath.

4. Stack the pages. Fold the construction paper cover in half. Place the riddles inside the cover and staple on the left side.

5. Write a title on the cover.

6. Share the book with classmates.

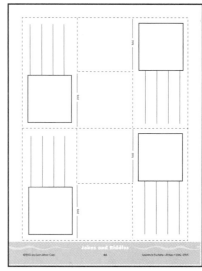

page 66

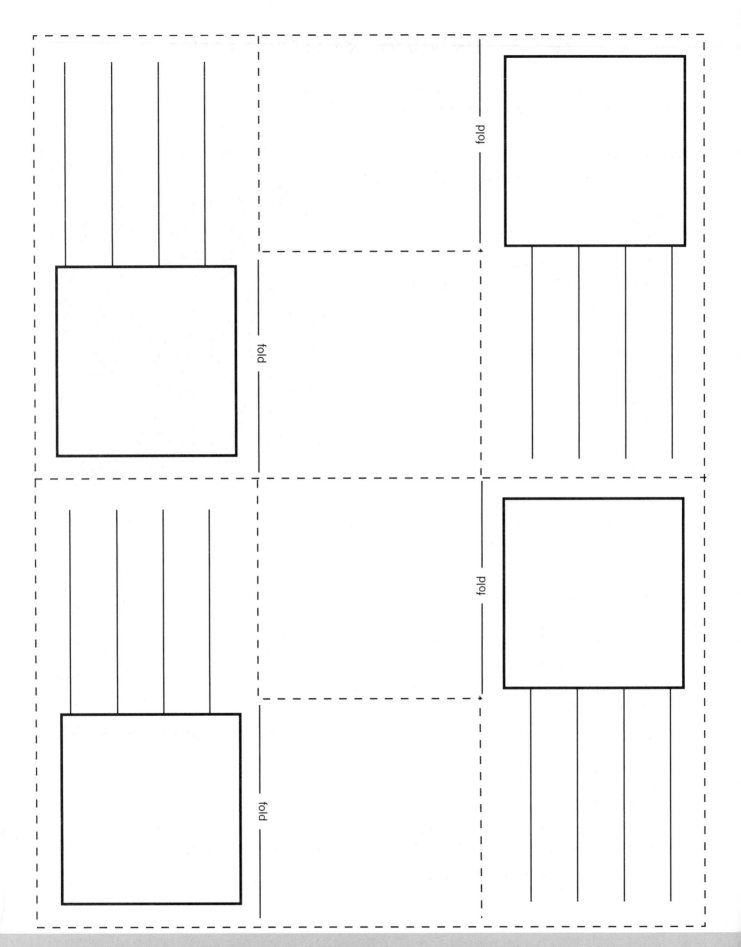

fold

fold

fold

The Little Book of Great Jokes

Everyone has favorite jokes. In this project, students combine four of their favorites in a small, but funny, book.

Materials

- two 5" x 8" (13 x 20 cm) pieces of construction paper
- ruler
- scissors
- colored pencils or marking pens
- five 3 1/2" x 4 1/2" (9 x 11.5 cm) sheets of writing paper
- glue
- stapler

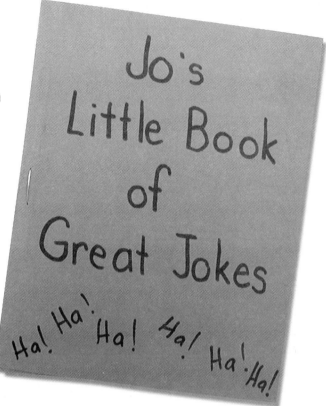

Steps to Follow

1. Fold each piece of construction paper in half as shown.

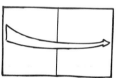

2. Draw a line to the center of the fold line as shown. Cut along this line. Repeat on the other piece of paper.

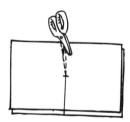

3. Slip the pieces of paper together along the cut lines. Fold the book closed.

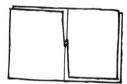

4. Write a joke on each piece of writing paper. Glue a joke on each of the inside pages. Add pictures if there is room. Staple the left-hand side to hold the pages together.

5. Design a cover on the front of the booklet.

Historical Fiction

Historical Fiction Bookmark.............. page 69
Make the bookmark following the instructions
on page 2. Review the description of the
genre and the reading list provided on the
bookmark. Then ask students to read at least
two examples of historical fiction.

Is It Historical Fiction? .... page 70
Review the attributes of historical fiction.
Students list the books they read and
then evaluate each book by checking the
appropriate boxes on the form.

A Friendly Letter .... pages 71 and 72
Students write a letter to a friend summarizing
and evaluating a historical fiction book they
read.

A Time Line........................ pages 73 and 74
Students make a time line of the important
events that occurred in the story they read.

Paint a Portrait....................pages 75 and 76
Students paint a portrait of the main character
from a book of historical fiction. Then they
write a descriptive paragraph about that
character.

Historical Fiction

Historical fiction is a kind of realistic fiction based on a historical period or event. It may portray real people in invented situations or invented people in historical settings. The time and place of the setting are portrayed authentically.

©2001 by Evan-Moor Corp • EMC 2703

- *Abigail Takes the Wheel* by Avi
- *Dear Levi: Letters From the Overland Trail* by Elvira Woodruff
- *Folks Call Me Appleseed John* by Andrew Glass
- *I Thought My Soul Would Rise and Fly* by Joyce Hansen
- *Ida Early Comes Over the Mountain* by Robert Burch
- *Jim Ugly* by Sid Fleischman
- *Lily's Crossing* by Patricia Reilly Giff
- *Little Farm in the Ozarks* by Roger Lea MacBride
- *Lucy's Wish* by Joan Lowery Nixon
- *Shakespeare's Scribe* by Gary L. Blackwood
- *The Night Crossing* by Karen Ackerman
- *The Watsons Go to Birmingham* by Christopher Paul Curtis

_____

_____

_____

Historical Fiction

©2001 by Evan-Moor Corp • EMC 2703

Name:

Is It Historical Fiction?

Write the title and author of each book you read. Make a check mark under the characteristics that are true about the book.

Name of Book	time and place of setting is real	real characters—invented events	invented characters—historical events
1 Title: _____ Author: _____			
2 Title: _____ Author: _____			
3 Title: _____ Author: _____			
4 Title: _____ Author: _____			
5 Title: _____ Author: _____			
6 Title: _____ Author: _____			

A Friendly Letter

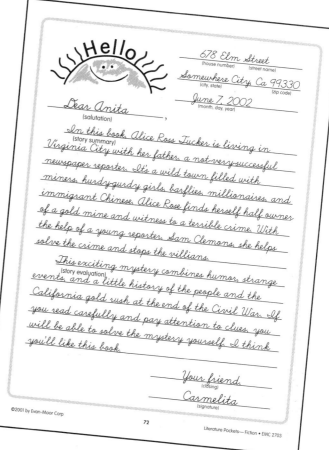

Students use the format of a friendly letter to report on a historical fiction book.

Materials

- page 72, reproduced for each student
- pencil
- envelope
- stickers to use for stamps

Steps to Follow

1. After reading a book of historical fiction, students write a letter summarizing and evaluating the book they read. Write these reminders on the chalkboard.

   The letter should include:

   - who the book was about

   - where and when the story took place

   - the most important events in the story

   - why your friend should or should not read the book

2. Students address an envelope and put a sticker in the corner for a stamp.

3. Allow time for students to share their letters. Then they place their letters in their pocket books.

Historical Fiction

Hello

_____
(house number)   (street name)

_____
(city, state)   (zip code)

_____
(month, day, year)

_____ ,
(salutation)

_____
(story summary)

_____

_____

_____

_____

_____

_____
(story evaluation)

_____

_____

_____

_____

_____
(closing)

_____
(signature)

A Time Line

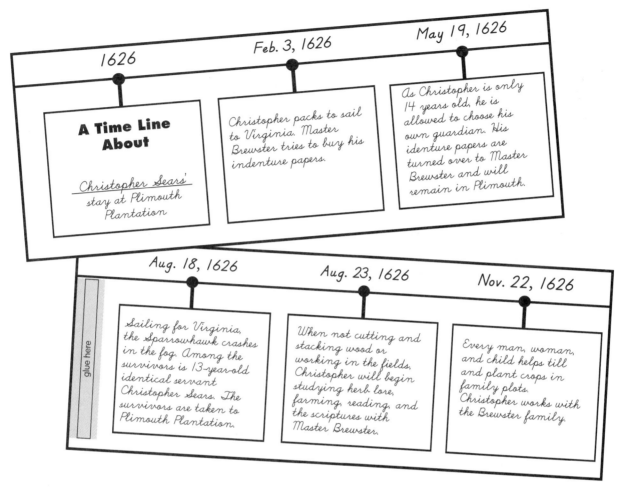

1626

A Time Line About

<u>Christopher Sears'</u> stay at Plimouth Plantation

Feb. 3, 1626

Christopher packs to sail to Virginia. Master Brewster tries to buy his indenture papers.

May 19, 1626

As Christopher is only 14 years old, he is allowed to choose his own guardian. His indenture papers are turned over to Master Brewster and will remain in Plimouth.

glue here

Aug. 18, 1626

Sailing for Virginia, the Sparrowhawk crashes in the fog. Among the survivors is 13-year-old identical servant Christopher Sears. The survivors are taken to Plimouth Plantation.

Aug. 23, 1626

When not cutting and stacking wood or working in the fields, Christopher will begin studying herb lore, farming, reading, and the scriptures with Master Brewster.

Nov. 22, 1626

Every man, woman, and child helps till and plant crops in family plots. Christopher works with the Brewster family.

Students recall important events from a story they read. Then they record the events in order on a time line, including dates if any were given.

Materials

- page 74, reproduced for each student
- scissors
- glue
- writing paper

Steps to Follow

1. On writing paper, make a list of the most important events that occurred in the story. The last item should be the concluding episode in the book.

2. Prepare the time line form by cutting the strips apart and gluing them end to end. If more than six spaces are needed, add additional strips to make the time line as long as necessary.

3. Write the events on the time line in the correct order. Include a date if possible (May 6, mid-June), if not, include the time of year (summer, late fall) or the book chapter (chapter 1, mid-chapter 3).

Historical Fiction

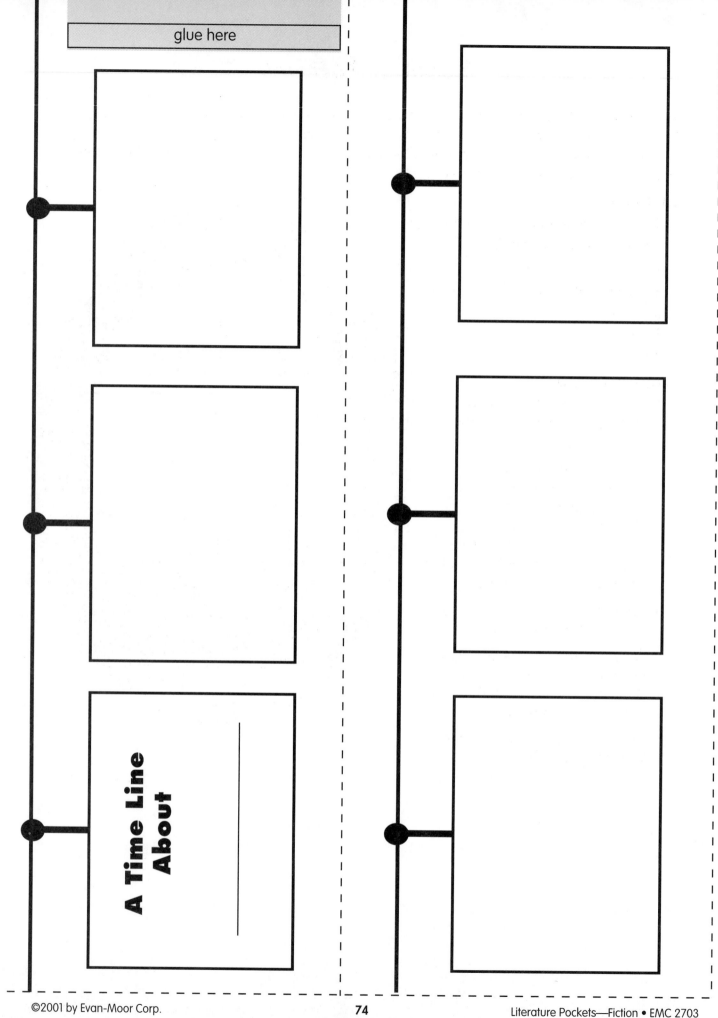

glue here

A Time Line About
_____

Paint a Portrait

Visit a historical home or a museum from earlier times and you will find portraits of people living at that time. Sometimes these are famous men and women from history, but often they are just family members. In this activity, students select a character from the book they read and then draw the person's portrait.

Materials

- page 76, reproduced for each student
- colored pencils or marking pens
- gold marking pens
- writing paper, cut in the shape of the frame
- scissors
- glue

Steps to Follow

1. Write the person's name on the white name plate at the bottom of the frame.

2. Select a character from the historical fiction read and draw a portrait (head and shoulders) of the person. Students may need to use their imaginations as well as story details in deciding what the person looks like.

3. Use gold marking pens to outline the design on the frame.

4. Write a paragraph describing the person drawn. This should be a description of the person's character, not physical appearance.

5. Glue the descriptive paragraph to the back of the portrait.

Samual Clemens

 Literature Pockets—Fiction • EMC 2703

Poetry

Poetry Bookmark .... **page 78**
Make the bookmark following the instructions on page 2. Review the description of the genre and the reading list provided on the bookmark. Then ask students to read at least two books of poetry.

Is It Poetry? .... **page 79**
Review the attributes of poetry books. Students list the books they read and then evaluate each book by checking the appropriate boxes on the form.

Poetry Book Report .... **page 80**
Using the form on page 80, students evaluate one of the poetry books they read.

Shape Poem .... **page 81**
Shape poems allow students to play with words in unusual ways as they create a poem and picture at the same time.

A Poetry Anthology .... **page 82**
Students make their own poetry anthologies. They collect their favorite poems, copy them neatly, and then illustrate the poems in interesting or colorful ways.

Poetry

Poetry has beautiful or powerful language carefully chosen for its meaning, sound, and rhythm. Poetry is imaginative and evokes strong emotions. Often, but not always, poetry has rhyming words.

- *A Pizza the Size of the Sun* by Jack Prelutsky
- *Balloons: and Other Poems* by Deborah Chandra
- *The Basket Counts* by Arnold Adoff
- *Big Talk: Poems for Four Voices* by Paul Fleischman
- *Bing, Bang, Boing: Poems and Drawings* by Douglas Florian
- *The Block* by Langston Hughes
- *Casey at the Bat* by Ernest Lawrence Thayer
- *Celebrate America In Poetry and Art* edited by Nora Panzer
- *Classic Poems to Read Aloud* edited by James Berry
- *Falling Up* by Shel Silverstein
- *Ogden Nash's Zoo* by Ogden Nash
- *Sad Underwear and Other Complications* by Judith Viorst

_____

_____

_____

_____

Poetry

©2001 by Evan-Moor Corp • EMC 2703

Name: _____

Is It Poetry?

Write the title and author of each book you read. Make a check mark under the characteristics that are true about the book.

Name of Book	beautiful language	powerful language	imaginative	raises strong emotions	the poems rhyme	the poems don't rhyme
1 Title: _____ Author: _____						
2 Title: _____ Author: _____						
3 Title: _____ Author: _____						
4 Title: _____ Author: _____						
5 Title: _____ Author: _____						
6 Title: _____ Author: _____						

Literature Pockets—Fiction • EMC 2703

Name: _____

Poetry Book Report

Which poetry book did you read? _____
title of book

Were all of the poems written by the same author?   Yes   No

Did someone collect poems written by different
authors and put them together?   Yes   No

If yes, write the name of the collector here. _____
name of collector

Was there a theme to the poems in the collection?   Yes   No

If yes, write the theme here. _____
theme

Were there illustrations in the poetry book?   Yes   No

Copy your favorite poem from this book in your best handwriting.

_____

_____

_____

_____

_____

_____

~ Poetry ~

Shape Poem

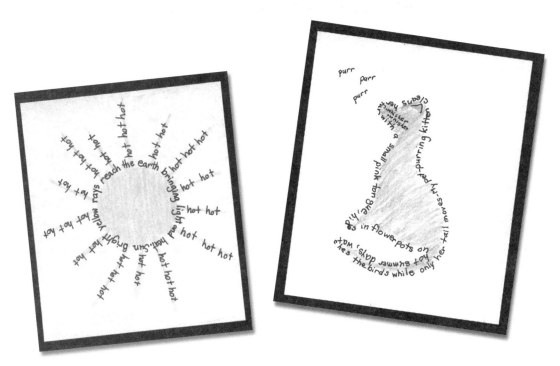

Sometimes it is fun to play with words in unusual ways to create a poem. Shape poems provide students an opportunity for this type of experience.

Material

- 2 pieces of copier paper
- black crayon or marking pen
- paper clip
- writing paper
- 9" x 12" (23 x 30.5 cm) colored construction paper
- glue

Steps to Follow

1. Explain that a shape poem follows the outline of a picture of the poem's subject. Draw a simple example on the chalkboard as a model.

2. Students select a simple object as a topic.

3. They make a list of words and phrases that describe the appearance and characteristics of the topic. Select the best ones and arrange them so they have a pleasing sound.

4. Using black crayon or marking pen, draw an outline shape of the object. Place a sheet of copier paper over the drawing. Fasten the pages together with a paper clip.

5. Write the words or phrases following the shape of the object to create the "shape" poem. Remove the top sheet of paper to see the completed poem.

6. Glue the completed poem to a sheet of colored paper to frame the shape poem. If the poem is small, cut the construction paper to form a more appropriate frame.

Poetry

A Poetry Anthology

Students make their own poetry anthologies. The poems may be collected in small purchased notebooks or in books made by the students following the directions below.

Materials

- two 5" x 9" (13 x 23 cm) pieces of tagboard
- 11" x 12" (28 x 30.5 cm) colored butcher paper, wrapping paper, shelf paper, or cloth
- four 8 1/2" x 9" (21.5 x 23 cm) pieces of white paper
- needle
- white thread
- glue
- cellophane tape

Steps to Follow—Make the Book

1. Lay the colored paper or cloth on a desk.

2. Center the tagboard pieces on the paper or cloth. Leave a small space between the two pieces. Mark the corner positions of the tagboard. Lift the tagboard and apply glue. Glue the tagboard in place.

3. Fold in the corners as shown. Glue or tape them in place.

4. Fold the paper or cloth in over the tagboard. Glue or tape all sides in place.

5. Fold the plain white paper in half. Sew the pieces together along the fold line.

6. The first and last pages will form the endsheets of the book. Put glue around the edges of the top piece of paper. Lay this centered on the left-hand inside cover. The sewn edge of the pages need to fit into the space left between the tagboard pieces. Put glue on the last piece of paper and press it onto the right-hand inside cover.

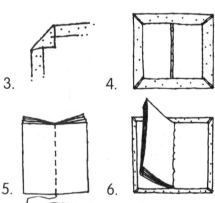

Steps to Follow—Collecting Poems

1. Discuss possible ideas for student collections. Will there be a certain type of poem—haiku, limericks, couplets? Will there be a theme—animal poems, poems about feelings, a mixture of poems?

2. Students determine the type of poems that will go in their anthologies. They copy one poem per page and illustrate it. (This will need to be done over a period of time as students read various poetry books.)

3. Write a title on the cover.

Poetry

Humorous Stories

Humorous Stories Bookmark............ page 84

Make the bookmark following the instructions on page 2. Review the description of the genre and the reading list provided on the bookmark. Then ask students to read at least two humorous stories.

Is It a Humorous Story? .... page 85

Review the attributes of humorous stories. Students list the books they read and then evaluate each book by checking the appropriate boxes on the form.

Laughter Scale .... page 86

Working together or as individuals, students develop a list of words or phrases to describe how funny a story is (made me smile, giggled out loud, fell down laughing, etc.). They write their descriptions from least funny to most funny using the form on page 86. Then students color in spaces to show how high up the "Laughter Scale" they would rate the humorous story they read. Extend the activity by having students write a paragraph on the back of the paper explaining why they gave the book that rating.

Comic Strip .... page 87

After reading a humorous story, students retell a favorite incident in comic strip form.

Humorous Stories

The characters, dialog, setting, and/or events may be realistic or imaginative. They are often combined with other genres. Whatever the stories contain, they are funny!

©2001 by Evan-Moor Corp • EMC 2703

- *A Year with Butch and Spike* by Gail Gauthier
- *Anastasia Absolutely* by Lois Lowry
- *Bug Boy* by Carol Sonenklar
- *Cockroach Cooties* by Laurence Yep
- *Dominic* by William Steig
- *Frindle* by Andrew Clements
- *I Was a Rat!* by Philip Pullman
- *Matilda* by Roald Dahl
- *Nasty, Stinky Sneakers* by Eve Bunting
- *The Best School Year Ever* by Barbara Robinson
- *The Hoboken Chicken Emergency* by Daniel Pinkwater
- *Wayside School Gets a Little Stranger* by Louis Sachar

_____

_____

_____

_____

Humorous Stories

©2001 by Evan-Moor Corp • EMC 2703

Name: _____

Is It a Humorous Story?

Write the title and author of each book you read. Make a check mark under the characteristics that are true about the book.

Name of Book	funny dialog	funny characters	funny events	combined with another genre
1 Title: _____ Author: _____				
2 Title: _____ Author: _____				
3 Title: _____ Author: _____				
4 Title: _____ Author: _____				
5 Title: _____ Author: _____				
6 Title: _____ Author: _____				

Literature Pockets—Fiction • EMC 2703

Name: _____

Laughter Scale

Fill in the words describing how funny your book was.
Write the least funny word or phrase at the bottom of
the scale and the most funny word or phrase at the top
near the bell. Then color the pole to show how you would
rate the book.

6 — _____

5 — _____

4 — _____

3 — _____

2 — _____

1 — _____

title of book

Humorous Fiction

Comic Strip

Students draw a comic strip to depict one of the highlights of a humorous story they read.

Materials

- two 4" x 12" (10 x 30.5 cm) pieces of white construction paper
- crayons, colored pencils, or marking pens
- glue
- ruler

Steps to Follow

1. Discuss the attributes of a comic strip (short, colorful, funny, pictures tell much of the story).

2. After reading a story, students select one humorous situation to retell in comic strip form. They plan the pictures and dialog for each part of their comic strips.

3. Students divide their paper into three 4" (10 cm) boxes. Outline each box with black crayon or marking pen. Glue the strips together. (Cut off any boxes not needed, or glue on more boxes if necessary.)

4. Draw a picture in each box. Add speech bubbles. Write dialog in the speech bubbles. Add short captions where needed to move the situation along.

5. Provide time for students to share their comic strips. Ask them to explain why they selected that situation to retell.

Humorous Fiction

Fantasy

Fantasy Bookmark .... page 89
Make the bookmark following the instructions on page 2. Review the description of the genre and the reading list provided on the bookmark. Then ask students to read at least two fantasy stories.

Is It Fantasy? .... page 90
Review the attributes of fantasy stories. Students list the books they read and then evaluate each book by checking the appropriate boxes on the form.

Fantasy Book Report .... page 91
Students complete the form on page 91 to report on a fantasy book they read.

Magic Wand .... page 92
Provide an assortment of craft materials and set students' imaginations free to make magic wands. They then write about how they would use their wand if it truly were magical.

Create a Game .... pages 93–96
Students create board games around a fantastic location from one of the fantasy books they read.

Fantasy

Make-believe and animals or inanimate objects that talk are important parts of a fantasy story. Some or all of the story elements (characters, setting, problem, solution, and events) are imaginative and would be impossible in the real world.

- *A Wizard of Earthsea* by Ursula K. LeGuin
- *The Black Cauldron* by Lloyd Alexander
- *Ella Enchanted* by Gail Carson Levine
- *The Five Sisters* by Margaret Mahy
- *Gulliver in Lilliput* by Margaret Hodges
- *The Hobbit, or, There and Back Again* by J. R. R. Tolkien
- *The Indian in the Cupboard* by Lynne Reid Banks
- *The Last of the Really Great Whangdoodles* by Julie Edwards
- *The Lion, the Witch, and the Wardrobe* by C. S. Lewis
- *Perloo the Bold* by Avi
- *Redwall* by Brian Jacques
- *Under the Cat's Eye* by Gillian Rubinstein
- *Well Wished* by Franny Billingsley

_____

_____

_____

_____

Fantasy

Name: _____

Is It Fantasy?

Write the title and author of each book you read. Make a check mark under the characteristics that are true about the book.

Name of Book	make-believe story events	fantasy setting invented events	animals or inanimate objects that talk	real-world setting— impossible events
1 Title: _____ Author: _____				
2 Title: _____ Author: _____				
3 Title: _____ Author: _____				
4 Title: _____ Author: _____				
5 Title: _____ Author: _____				
6 Title: _____ Author: _____				

Literature Pockets—Fiction • EMC 2703

Note: Reproduce this page for each student to use with "Fantasy Book Report" on page 88.

Name: _____

Title of the book _____

Author _____

List three fantastic/magical events that occurred in the story.

1. _____

2. _____

3. _____

Describe your favorite character in the story.

_____

_____

_____

_____

Would you recommend this book to a friend? Why or why not?

_____

_____

_____

Magic Wand

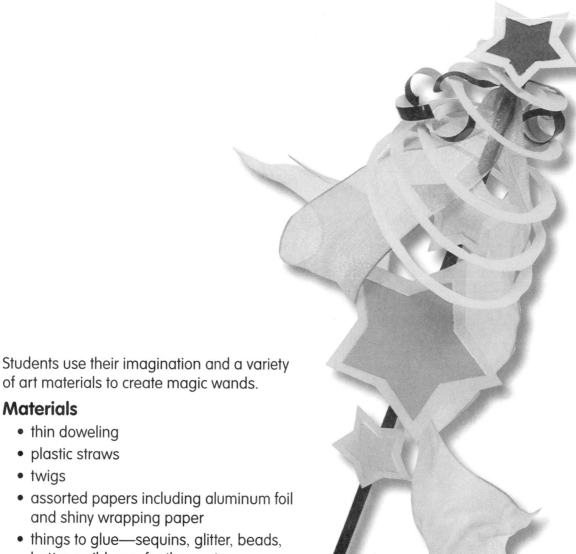

Students use their imagination and a variety of art materials to create magic wands.

Materials

- thin doweling
- plastic straws
- twigs
- assorted papers including aluminum foil and shiny wrapping paper
- things to glue—sequins, glitter, beads, buttons, ribbons, feathers, etc.
- scissors
- glue
- tape
- marking pens
- writing paper

Steps to Follow

1. Establish procedures students are to follow in collecting materials from a central location.

2. Discuss possible ways to decorate a magic wand. Show the types of materials students choose to use.

3. Students collect materials and decorate their wands.

4. When the wands are completed, students write about one way in which they would use their wands if they were really magic.

Fantasy

Create a Game

Students create a board game for the story they read. The theme of the game should relate to the theme of the story (finding something magical, a quest, an adventurous journey, escaping from a wizard or dragon, etc.). The board should reflect the setting of the story. The playing pieces should relate to the characters in the story.

Materials

- sample game boards
- pages 94–96, reproduced for each student
- 20″ x 16″ (51 x 40.5 cm) tagboard
- scissors
- glue
- crayons or marking pens
- assorted items to use for game pieces—beans, buttons, pebbles, counters, etc.
- dice—optional

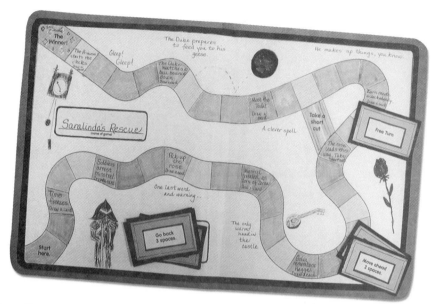

Steps to Follow—Planning the Game

1. Examine some board games to determine what elements each one contains. Ask students to identify the theme of the game and describe how the game board and playing pieces reflect this theme.

2. Display a fantasy story that was read aloud to the class or one that most students are familiar with. Ask students to think of types of board games that might be made that could relate to the story. Write their ideas on the chalkboard. Include a discussion of what the board and playing pieces might look like and what rules would apply.

3. Then each student plans a game that relates to the fantasy book he or she read.

Steps to Follow—Making the Board

The following directions are for using the game forms on pages 94–96. Some students may want to create their own game board.

1. Glue the two parts of the game board to a sheet of tagboard.

2. While the glue is drying, cut out the cards for the game. Make additional cards if needed to play the game.

3. Write the game rules on the form.

4. After the glue dries, write the name on the game board and color in the background. Glue the game rules to the back of the board.

page 96

Fantasy

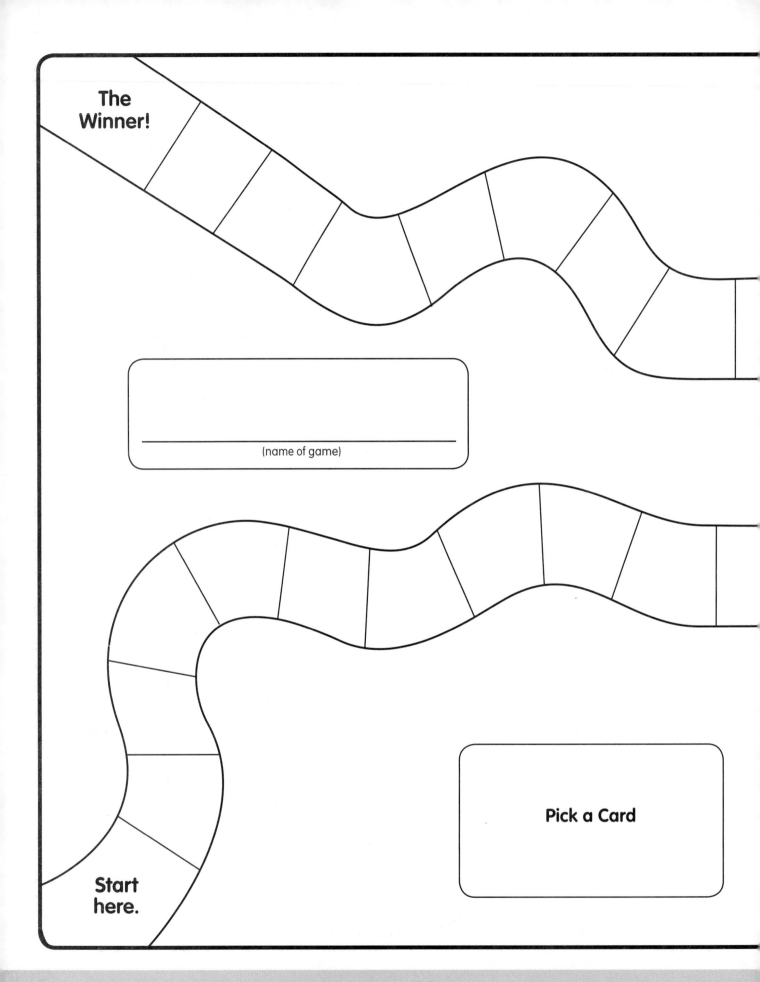

The Winner!

_____
(name of game)

Pick a Card

Start here.

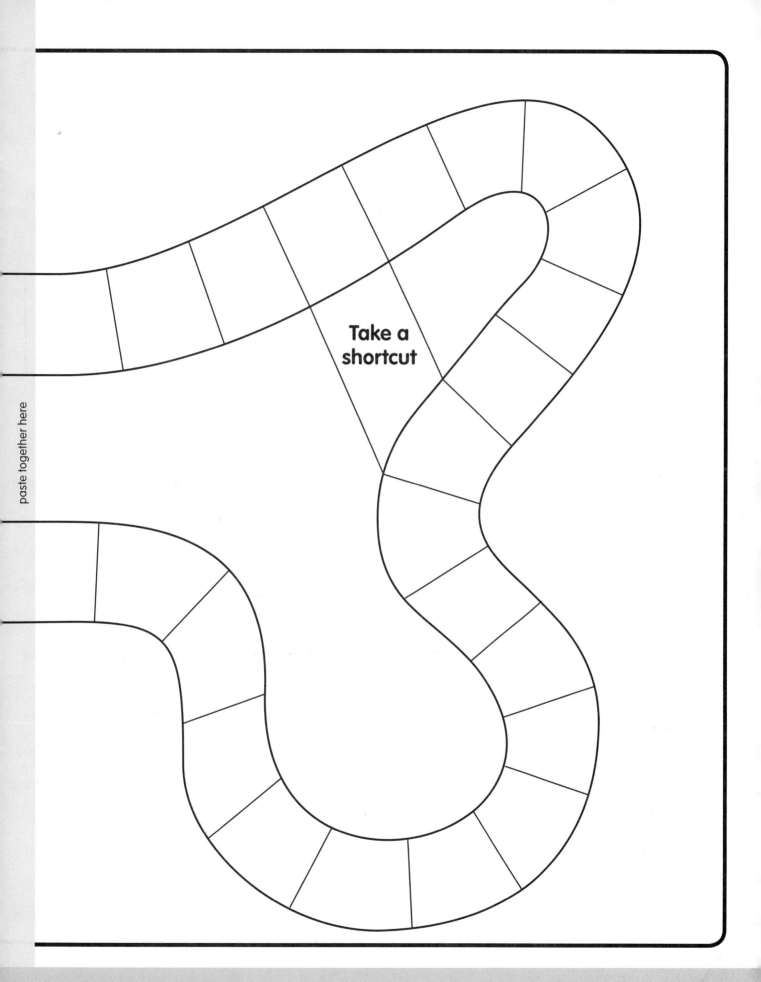

paste together here

Take a
shortcut

Fantasy

My Game

_____
(name of game)

Number of Players: _____

Rules: _____

_____

_____

_____

_____

_____

_____

Lose 1 turn.	Lose 1 turn.	Go back 3 spaces.
Free Turn	Free Turn	Go back 1 space.
Move ahead 2 spaces.	Move ahead 1 space.	Pick another card.

Fantasy